MW01488954

The Healing POWER of Peace

TWENTY THIRD 23rd PUBLICATIONS

Twenty-Third Publications
A Division of Bayard
One Montauk Avenue, Suite 200
New London, CT 06320
(860) 437-3012 or (800) 321-0411
www.twentythirdpublications.com
ISBN:1-58595-535-3

The Scripture passages contained herein are from the *New Revised
Standard Version of the Bible*, copyright ©1989, by the Division of
Christian Education of the National Council of Churches in the U.S.A.
All rights reserved.

Library of Congress Catalog Card Number: 2005929698
Printed in the U.S.A.

Contents

Why in the world can't we all get along? Why have we made enormous progress in all areas of our lives but not in the areas of war and peace? Why do we create enemies and keep them? Why after all these centuries of different religious experiences and great philosophies, do our hearts and our world still fail to find peace? Why are morning, noon, and evening news broadcasts so filled with stories of shooting, rape, divorce, incest, infidelity, torture, stealing, and executions? Why do we seem to be a people and culture more interested in violence than peace and harmony? Why and why and why?

These are troubling and very difficult questions to answer. Instead of pretending to provide an easy prescription for such vast problems, this little book which is part of "The Healing Power" series, will focus on inviting the reader to reflect on the most important questions and on analyzing the causes and effects of peace in our lives. Together we will look at the marks of true peace: spiritual well-being, healing, and fullness of life.

It is heartening to notice that increasing numbers of people and organizations are devoting time, energy, studies, and action toward creating peaceful conditions in our world. Peace studies are increasingly included in the curriculum of many colleges and universities, and many governmental and nongovernmental institutions deal directly with the numerous facets of peace, survival, and quality of life on this planet. All are interested in peace that is enduring. Temporary peace or "peace" that results from nuclear deterrence is not what our hearts seek. History has shown again and again that that kind of peace will hold only as long as the circumstances remain the same. But circumstances never remain the same.

There must be, at a deeper level, something else that generates a driving force toward a peaceful world. The causes of peace should encompass ideas, attitudes, relationships, political, economic, and social realities that are conducive to creating and maintaining peace. Also, this peace should be based primarily on inner peace. World peace is a reflection of the peace within ourselves, with God, and with others. Peace mirrors our souls, minds, and hearts. Therefore, no lasting peace is possible if we are content with just external means. The truth is that nations do not make peace. Individuals do. Peace is not an abstract concept; it is a living experience.

Spiritual well-being, healing, and the fullness of life are the marks of true peace.

Transforming our own hearts and those of people all over the world may take time—perhaps a very long time, but it is the only way to achieve lasting peace. "If [we] do not change direction," says a Chinese proverb, "[we] are most likely to end up where [we] are going." By following the ways of conflict and anger, it is obvious that we are going to end up at war not at peace. If, as we often say, "everything has changed since September 11, 2001," why don't we also change our ways of thinking?

A new world order does not necessarily create a new consciousness. But a new consciousness does create a new world order. All it takes is a change of heart and mind in one person, and in another, and another, and another.

A new consciousness is urgently needed, one that looks forward to "the city that has foundations, whose architect and builder is God" (Heb 11:10) and whose inhabitants belong to a "new humanity" (Eph 2:15). It will be a special delight for me if this book contributes even a little toward the creation of this much-needed new consciousness.

CHAPTER ONE

The Prince of Peace

"Peace I leave with you; my peace I give to you. I do not give to you as the world gives."

■ JOHN 14:27

The boat, tossed mercilessly by the waves, was in grave danger. The disciples, in a state of high emergency, were struggling for their lives. But Jesus was resting calmly and peacefully. They woke him up and said to him, "Teacher, don't you care that we are perishing?" He stood up and rebuked the wind, and said to the sea, "Peace! Be still!" (Mk 4:38–39).

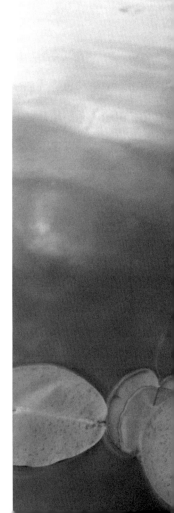

5

And peace there was.

Most, if not all of us, have experienced stormy times when we just wanted something to hold on to or someone who could help us to calm down and be at peace.

We know that peace is essential, because without it chaos, worries, and fear take over our lives. We know that without peace we are paralyzed by hurts, disappointments, and challenges. Only the command of Jesus, "Peace! Be still!" will calm the many storms that beat against the boats of our lives.

He Is Our Peace

Jesus came to bring peace to the world. We will know this peace when we, transformed by the Holy Spirit, reflect the likeness of God. The miracle of the Incarnation is that the Son of God wanted to be any and every human being, and that there should be no one in whom we do not recognize God's presence.

All people have their gods, religions, philosophies, ideologies, and traditions. But Christians have something more: a living God. Jesus Christ is not an abstract concept or a kind of an ideology that can eventually lead to some action. Jesus of Nazareth who was crucified, died, and raised from the dead is the Lord and Savior of the world. "He is our peace" (Eph

2:14), wrote St. Paul. He is so, not as a pacifist movement or an abstract ideal, but because he is, as Peter called him, "The Messiah, the Son of the living God" (Mt 16:16). His teachings are summed up as follows:

- "You shall love the Lord your God with all your heart, and with all your soul, and with all your mind" (Mt 22:37). This means that we should love God completely and not pick and choose what is convenient for us from his commandments.

- "You shall love your neighbor as yourself" (Mt 22:39).

- "Love your enemies" (Mt 5:44). This means, in Gandhi's terms, that we should "oppose evil, not the evil-doer."

- "Leave your gift there before the altar and go; first be reconciled to your brother or sister, and then come and offer your gift" (Mt 5:24). So, reconciliation is more important than any gift offered to God.

- Turn the other cheek. Go the extra mile. No retaliation. No getting even. No eye for an eye and tooth for a tooth (see Mt 5:38–41).

- "Do to others as you would have them do to you" (Lk 6:31).

- Whatever is done for another person, it is done for the Lord himself (see Mt 5:25–46).

- "Love one another as I have loved you" (Jn 15:12). Note that if Jesus stopped at "Love one another," he would not have given us anything new; other religions already have this. "As I have loved you" suggests that we are supposed to be ready to die for others as he died for us. He was love incarnate. Such love does not discriminate; it is all-embracing. Now we come a little closer to understanding why Jesus can say, "Peace I leave with you; my peace I give you" (Jn 14:27).

Accepting the peace of Jesus means that you are not lonely when you are alone. You are forgiven when you err. You are secure when you face danger. You have shelter when you feel homeless. You have food on the table when you are hungry. You are helped when you are in need. You are safe when you feel threatened. You are liberated when you are overwhelmed by a sinful or frustrating past. You are comforted when you grieve. You are at peace when you are tossed by life's storms. When you accept the peace of Jesus, you are

Jesus asks us to accept his peace and share it with others.

able to trust God regardless of your circumstances. You believe God's promises, and you count on the unconditional divine love.

For those times when you forget about the peace of Jesus, visit the following Gospel passages:

- If you are burdened and weary, visit Matthew 11:25–30.

- If you are anxious and worried, visit Matthew 6:19–34.

- If you lack faith, visit Mark 4:35–41.

- If your heart is troubled, visit John 14.

- If you need healing from an illness, visit Mark 5:25–34.

- If you doubt that Jesus is with you, visit John 6:16–21.

Just turn any problem over to Jesus and the Holy Spirit, and you will see the needed result. Perhaps you will not see an instant end of a conflict, but you will realize that the Sermon on the Mount is not a utopian ideal. It was meant for a real world—a world of flawed social and spiritual structures. Jesus does not ask us to love a beautiful abstract concept. He asks us to love one another in this sinful world, here and now. He asks us to accept his peace and share it with others. "Blessed are the peacemakers, for they shall be called the children of God" (Mt 5:9).

Does this mean we will always be successful? Probably not. Jesus himself did not succeed in winning the heart of his enemies, even though he was the most loving man who ever lived. Instead, he was hated, humiliated, and crucified. He knew also that those who practice his way of life will be taken advantage of, exploited, and persecuted, "For if you love those who love you," he said, "what reward do you have?" (Mt 5:46), and assured them, "Blessed are you when people revile you and persecute you...on my account....Your reward is great in heaven" (Mt 5:11–12). This suggests that even peace, which is by itself a noble cause, should not be the focus of our seeking. The real focus is Jesus himself. Only when we truly seek him will we find peace because peace is first an interior gift. The good we do does not give us the inner peace that can be found only in Jesus—good personified and the source of all good. "For he is our peace," insists Paul, "he has broken down the dividing wall, that is, the hostility between us" (Eph 2:14).

The peace of Christ is essentially inner peace, and inner peace cannot be found except in God. St.

Augustine's famous line, "Our hearts are restless until they rest in you," reminds us of this truth. Every one of us feels unrest and disturbance when we deviate from the path God assigns to us. We are unhappy until we return to that path.

Inner peace usually has three aspects to it: 1. We are on a solid foundation—Christ; 2. we act according to the values Christ has taught us; 3. we let our inner harmony take over conflicts and divisions.

Once our inner peace is established, it will naturally and necessarily lead to outward peace. How can it be otherwise? The inner struggle for the kingdom of God will become visible and tangible in the struggle for reconciliation with others and for peace at all levels. Those who have inner peace cannot help but radiate God's peace. Their weapons are not the weapons used by their adversaries, but the weapons of light. Their fight is not fought only in their own interests, but in the interests of their adversaries as well.

Such "warfare" does not conquer and humiliate our adversaries. It redeems them and gives them serenity, peace, and wholeness. It makes us attend to others according to God's will, not our own. Christ's peace is a conversion of the heart to God and to one another. Christ, not us, makes this peace possible. God's "last word" is Jesus Christ. "This is my Son, the Beloved; with him I am well pleased; listen to him!" (Mt 17:5).

The Role of Jesus

Jesus' life, like his teachings, ran counter to the status quo and to culturally-accepted attitudes. Obsessed by the reality of the kingdom of God he wanted to establish, he did not care about settling down, having a good job, getting married, having a large house, a respected position in the community, well-connected friends, or money. Instead, he chose to spend his time with outcasts, criminals, the sick, prostitutes, and, above all, the poor. He wanted social relationships based on service and humility, not on domination and exploitation. He wanted truthfulness in religious activities, not hypocrisy. He could not stand the well-established scribes and Pharisees, whom he chastised: "Woe to you, scribes and Pharisees, hypocrites…. You snakes, you brood of vipers! How can you escape being sentenced to hell?" (Mt 23:23, 33). When Jesus saw something wrong, he confronted it publicly, without fear, and without compromise. "I have not come to bring peace, but a sword" (Mt 10:34), he said, the sword of truth.

No matter what their positions or status, all

those who do not follow the laws of love, justice, and truthfulness are going to see Jesus as a threat. He was a threat in his time; he was a threat throughout the centuries; and he is still a threat now. When his ideas infect people, patterns change, structures crack, and false leaders crumble.

He had to be stopped in his day and people try to stop his followers today because authority figures fear radical change. The soul of his strategy will never change, however, at any time in human history. His message can't be stopped. "You shall love your neighbor as yourself" (Mt 22:39); "Love one another as I have loved you" (Jn 15:12); "Love your enemies" (Mt 5:44); and "The truth will make you free" (Jn 8:32). This is the divine constitution for the kingdom of God and for peace—a true peace.

For people of faith, peacemaking is not an optional activity. It is a must. Unity and peace should be high priorities in our lives because they are of paramount importance to God. They even take precedence over prayer. Jesus said: "Leave your gift there before the altar and go and be reconciled first to your brother or sister; then come and offer your gift" (Mt 5:24).

Christians must be at peace and work for peace everywhere they can. Recall once again, Jesus' words,

"Blessed are the peacemakers, for they will be called the children of God" (Mt 5:9).

Christians must be at peace and work for peace everywhere they can.

This is exactly what the Church of Christ is supposed to practice and teach. The saints were a living example of this. They were genuine peacemakers. They radiated peace in their own lives, and they tried to bring peace wherever they went.

It is remarkable to see how much emphasis has been placed on peace, especially in the modern era by papal teaching, by the Second Vatican Council, and by various pastoral letters of bishops' conferences all over the world.

Pacem in Terris, the encyclical written in 1963 by Pope John XXIII, who was one of the greatest spiritual and social influences of the twentieth century, attracted the attention of the whole world and won a universal hearing. It did so because for the first time a pope was addressing the whole world and "all men of good will," and also because the message in this encyclical responded to a deep desire in everyone's heart.

A Message of Peace

Pope John XXIII's profound intuition was that the human spirit would animate global and comprehensive relationships. This same intuition defined the conditions for peace which were truth, justice, love, and freedom.

Pope John's message was a popular one because it focused on the rights and duties of the human person, delivering a responsible reminder that to every right there corresponds a duty: "For every fundamental human right draws its indestructible moral force from natural law, which, in granting it, imposes a corresponding obligation" (30).

The pope also condemned the arms race and delivered a critical comment toward nuclear war saying: "It is hardly possible to imagine that in the atomic era, war could be used as an instrument of justice" (127).

Commenting on *Pacem in Terris*, Pope John Paul II said the following inspiring words:

Blessed Pope John XXIII was not afraid of the future. He was sustained in his optimism by his deep trust in God and in man, both of which grew out of the sturdy climate of faith in which he had grown up. Moved by his trust in Providence, even in what seemed like a permanent situation of conflict, he did not hesitate to summon the leaders of his time to a new vision of the world. This is the legacy that he left us.

Pope Paul VI also spoke abundantly on the problem of war and violence and he made an impassioned plea for peace at the United Nations. "No more war, war never again! Never one against the other." These words still echo in the ears and hearts of all people of good will.

In his encyclical *Populorum Progressio* of 1967, Pope Paul VI expressed his desire to enhance human dignity through reform of structural and social conditions. This would eliminate the very causes of injustice, which he hoped would then decrease the enmity between nations. In his 1978 message to the United Nations, he said:

Resource to arms is a scandalous thing. The thought of disarmament on the other hand awakens great hope. The disproportion between the resources of money and mind that are put at the service of the dead and those that are devoted to the service of life is a great scandal. The hope is that, as military expenditures lessen, a substantial part of the immense resources they preempt today may be used for a vast project of development on a world scale.

Pope John Paul II was an outspoken advocate for peace, perhaps even more than all his predecessors. Indeed, he did not spare any opportunity—and he had many of them during his long pontificate—to let the world know his views against war, preaching the necessity to build bridges between people not walls, make peace not war, and promote harmony not violence. Also, he did not believe that the arms race is a form of national security; but, rather, a threat to the peace of the world. Real peace should consist of working toward relieving hunger and suffering. Perhaps the essence of his thoughts on peace can be found in his encyclical *Redemptor Hominis*:

> We all know well that the areas of misery and hunger on our globe could have been made fertile in a short time if the gigantic investments for armaments at the service of war and destruction had been changed into investments for food at the service of life.

Real peace should consist of working toward relieving hunger and suffering.

For this reason the Church does not cease to implore each side of the two and to beg everybody in the name of God and in the name of man: do not kill! Do not prepare destruction and extermination for man! Think of your brothers and sisters who are suffering hunger and misery! Respect each one's dignity and freedom!

Also, at Christmas of 2003, he prayed:

Save us from the wars and armed conflict which lay waste whole areas of the world, from the scourge of terrorism and from the many forms of violence which assail the weak and the vulnerable. Save us from discouragement as we face the paths to peace, difficult paths indeed, yet possible and therefore necessary.

The Second Vatican Council, convened by Pope John XXIII, who wanted the Church to bring itself up to date and address the major questions of the day, had to address the issue of war. The Council issued the following condemnation:

"Any act of war aimed indiscriminately at the destruction of entire cities or of extensive areas along with their population is a crime against God and man himself. It merits unequivocal and unhesitating condemnation" (*Gaudium et Spes*, 80). This Council also linked peace to justice:

> Peace is not merely the absence of war. Nor can it be reduced solely to the maintenance of a balance of power between enemies. Nor is it brought about by dictatorship. Instead, it is rightly and appropriately called "an enterprise of justice" (Isa 32:7). Peace results from that harmony built into human society by its divine Founder, and actualized by men as they thirst after ever greater justice (*Gaudium et Spes*, 78).

Also, the Council called all Christians to work for peace:

> All Christians are urgently summoned "to practice the truth in love" (Eph 4:15) and to join with all true peacemakers in pleading for peace and bringing it about (*Gaudium et Spes*, 78).

In the footsteps of the Second Vatican Council, pastoral letters on war and peace were repeatedly issued by bishops everywhere, condemning violence and advocating the cause of peace and justice. A special mention should be given here to *The Challenge of Peace: God's Promise and Our Response,* a pastoral letter on war and peace written by the National

Conference of Catholic Bishops in May of 1983. At the beginning of this 138-page document, we read the following lines, which summarize the entire letter:

What are we saying? Fundamentally, we are saying that the decisions about nuclear weapons are among the most pressing moral questions of our age. While these decisions have obvious military and political aspects, they involve fundamental moral choices. In simple terms, we are saying that good ends (defending one's country, protecting freedom, etc.) cannot justify immoral means (the use of weapons which kill indiscriminately and threaten whole societies). We fear that our world and nation are headed in the wrong direction. More weapons with greater destructive potential are produced every day. More and more nations are seeking to become nuclear powers. In our quest for more and more security we fear we are actually becoming less and less secure.

Again, peacemaking for Christians is not an optional commitment or activity. It is a requirement, and it is so because of our faith. We are called to be peacemakers by Jesus Christ himself, and the definitions and contents of this peacemaking are not set by personal, ideological, and political agendas. They must be set and understood according to the Scripture and teachings of the Church, which is, according to the *Catechism of the Catholic Church*, "The sacrament of the unity of the human race and of its union with God" (2305). This is also the true goal of prophetic peace and a new world order.

FOR YOUR REFLECTION & RESPONSE

1. Jesus was considered a threat to the established powers of his day. Would he be considered a threat if he lived in any capital city of our world today? What would you do if your government required from you something contrary to God's way? What guidance can you draw from Jesus' teachings?

2. Many peacemakers were considered, as Martin Luther King, Jr. was, "troublemakers," because they used nonviolent tactics such as marches, demonstrations, boycotts, and, in some cases, civil disobedience. This was their way to make a point against war and to convince people and the government that peace never comes through war. Do you agree with them? If not, why not?

3. Does the Sermon on the Mount have an impact on your way of seeing the world? (See Mt 5:1–10.) Do you see the relevance of this sermon to today's violent struggles?

4. Read Ephesians 4:29–32. Put your life under St. Paul's scrutiny. Do you think, speak, or act in a way that may "grieve the Holy Spirit of God"? Are you kind and forgiving "as God in Christ has forgiven you"?

5. Jesus says: "Peace be with you" (Lk 24:36). By saying this, what does Jesus want his disciples as well as everyone of us to experience? Do you ever repeat Jesus' greeting when you meet others?

Affirmation

Repeat this several times a day.

I will let the peace of Christ within me move out, bringing harmony to all my relationships.

PRAYER

Dear God,

You are in heaven and on earth, everywhere and at all times. You are the light that dissipates all darkness.

Your will be done on earth as it is in heaven. May your light shine forth over the signs of the times and the darkness of the day.

Let your love control the events of history, transform our hatreds, and transfigure our hurts into paths to your kingdom.

Let your revelation awaken in us the sense of truth and justice.

Let your will enliven every cell of our being, and let your grace help us to be aware of the difference when we are doing things your way, or our way.

Help us understand that every war is a civil war, for every war is a war between brothers and sisters, and every war takes place within the mind and heart of every one of us first.

Forgive us, O merciful God, and give us the courage to forgive every one of our brothers and sisters. Let peace prevail everywhere, for you are our peace and you are everywhere. Amen.

CHAPTER TWO

In Pursuit of Peace

"Depart from evil, and do good;
seek peace, and pursue it."

■ PSALM 34:14

After all, it is all about security—personal, national, and world security, isn't it? We want to be free from fear, want, danger, and special care, don't we? Maybe this is why we are so determined in winning wars and so resolved in finding and maintaining peace. We want to be secure at all fronts.

But an honest look at our fears compels us to conclude that we are far from feeling secure. We fear weapons of mass destruction. We fear ter-

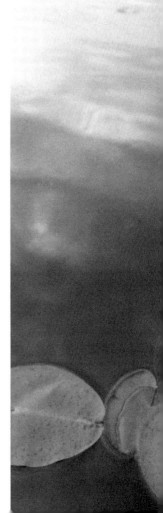

24

rorism. We fear the growing instability in our own society and in the world. We fear not being able to make it. We fear not being in charge. We fear our own selves and demons. And we declare war against the enemy, not knowing exactly who or what this enemy is, thinking that violence can abolish violence and that evil will be eliminated from the face of the earth by eliminating, if we can, the evildoers.

Such a strategy has borne some fruits throughout the centuries, but it has failed in the long run. Evil is still here, right now. After thousands of years of life on this planet, we are no closer to peace than were the tribes of ancient history. Since the beginning of time, we have been fighting each other. Why?

Causes of War

When human beings interact, conflicts always surface. Yet we cannot avoid this interaction. No one can survive in isolation. More and more we are realizing that we need each other, as individuals as well as nations. Self-sufficiency is an illusion. Moreover, it is impossible today to be unaffected by others, for good or ill, because we have instant access to information from every corner of the earth. Yet, this more often leads to war and conflict than to peace. What emotions drive us toward conflict?

The first thing that comes to mind is fear. We are not born afraid. We learn fear. Our parents, teachers, friends, and many others teach us to fear. And fear begets hostility. Out of love are born patience and peace. Out of fear are born hatred and hostility, which lead to war and violence. Thomas Merton observed rightly:

At the root of all war is fear, not so much the fear men have of one another as the fear they have of everything. It is not merely that they do not trust one another: they do not even trust themselves….They cannot trust anything because they have ceased to believe in God.

Other causes of wars that are directly or indirectly related to fear include racism, bigotry, nationalism, fanaticism, fundamentalism, greed, and lust for power. The apostle James wrote in his letter:

Those conflicts and disputes among you, where do they come from? Do they not come from your cravings that are at war within you? You want something and do not have it; so you commit murder. And you covet something and you cannot obtain it; so you engage in disputes and conflicts (Jas 4:1–2).

Ignorance can also be a cause for war. Even with the best intentions in the world (like liberation, salvation, values), kings, emperors, and presidents have declared war based on false information. They did not know the entire story or the other side of the story. They assumed that everything they do is good, and everything the other side does must be evil. Throughout history, ignorance has been responsible for many millions of innocent deaths. This is a fact.

Sometimes we "kill people who are killing people," as singer and activist Holly Near says, "to show that killing people is wrong." Violence has existed since the beginning of time. Remember the story of selfish Cain who murdered his innocent brother Abel? Violence is still here now. J. Krishnamurti (1895–1986), one of the world's great spiritual teachers, describes our reality with dreadful accuracy.

We are supposed to have lived on this earth for a million years, and during that long evolution, we have remained barbarians. We may be cleaner, quicker at communication, have better hygiene, transportation, and so on, but morally, ethically, and—if I may use the word—spiritually, we are still barbarians. We kill each other not only in war, but also by words, by gesture. We are very competitive. We are very ambitious….Self-interest is the dominant note in our life—concern with our well-being, security, possessions, power, and so on….Every country in the world…is gathering armaments—every country, however poor, however rich. It used to be a club that killed another, now we can vaporize millions with one atom bomb or neutron bomb….Ethically we are what we have been for a million years.

Some historians have estimated that, from the fifteenth century before Christ to this day, humankind has experienced peace on earth only for a total of about 300 years. The rest of the time war has been going on some place in the world. Indeed, the previous century, which should have been the most civilized because of our technological advances, has been the most bloody and violent of all previous centuries. Even though no one knows the exact number of lives lost through war, some estimates put the death toll for the twentieth century at 110 million casualties—compared with some 40 million killed in the preceding 900 years.

We can no longer consider any war as strictly a regional concern. "When peace has been broken anywhere," as Franklin Roosevelt put it, "the peace of all countries everywhere is in danger."

In this sad and dark context, can we still dare to talk about peace? It all depends on what we mean by the word "peace."

What Do We Mean by "Peace"?

"Peace" is an elusive term. People use it to cover a multitude of meanings. Look at the many ways we use "peace" in our everyday language, in phrases like "inner peace," "peace of mind," "world peace," "peace time," "peace at any price," "at peace," "Peace!" "I wish they'd leave me in peace," "go in peace," "peace treaty," "peaceful relations," "officer of the peace," "keeping the peace," "peacemaker," "making peace with God," "making peace with oneself," "a peaceful place," "the gift of peace," "peace be with you," "Prince of peace," and so on. The word "peace" is also used in the names of many institutions and organizations.

Moreover, in the name of "peace," injustices have been committed. For "peace," people have been oppressed, and wars have been fought. "Peace" has been used by imperial powers in the past and by global powers in modern times as a pretext to subdue others and rule them.

So peace can be an action to avoid war, or it can be a path to reconciliation, friendship, and an individual or national sense of well-being and security. But at the same time, peace can be used as a pretext for war, or in casual conversations, or in naïveté, or in camouflage, especially by those who cry: "'Peace, peace,' when there is no peace" (Jer 6:14).

The Greeks and the Romans who gave birth to our Western civilization also spoke about peace. *Eirene*, the Greek word for "peace," meant a truce between wars rather than the end of wars. *Pax*, the Latin word for "peace," pointed to a certain agreement or pact not to fight for the time being. But in both cases, war was an inevitable reality.

The Hebrew Scriptures use *shalom* for "peace," implying a stronger content, as does the Arabic word *salam*, which is different from the word *hudna* (temporary truce). *Shalom* refers more toward "wholeness" and "completeness." One is at peace when one becomes the person God intended him or her to be. War is rejected because it makes us less human. Although *shalom* was an important word in the Bible, the people of Israel realized that they failed to achieve wholeness according to God's intention. So they had to struggle down through the centuries. *Shalom*, then, does not seem to be meant for the time being, but it will certainly be at the end as it was in the beginning. The sad reality is that we have, in human history, successive *hudnas* or truces rather than *salam, shalom,* true peace. This is simply a fact.

> We are at peace when we become what God wants us to be.

The word "peace," as we have seen, is used in a wide variety of ways, driven by diverse assumptions, perceptions, and practices. Since it can be all these things, our conceptions of it are tied to the way we perceive the nature of being human and the meaning of life itself.

To understand what peace is for us today in a more specific and clear way, it will be very helpful to first shine a light on what peace is not.

What Peace Is Not

Peace is not just the absence of hostility. It is not just a negative conception—absence of war, end of fighting, draft resistance, getting the troops out of an occupied country.

Peace is not only a cessation of physical killing; it is also a cessation of slow killing through structural violence and unjust economic and social conditions.

Killing another human being can be done not only with a gun, but also by denying the person's humanity through oppression, abuse, indifference, or invasion and manipulation. These are daily occurrences that should draw the attention of peacemakers.

Peace is not just a kind of tranquility that indicates the absence of tension that makes life more bearable. Indeed, tranquility—complete harmony and accord—is sometimes equated with a lack of zest for life and for growth and development. Such "peace" is only stagnation, similar to the peace of the grave—peace in which the dead are said to be resting.

Compromising the truth out of love of comfort, lack of courage, or sheer cowardly acquiescence is not "peace." The path to true peace involves more than defending one's rights. Truth, goodness, and peace should travel the same path. To do nothing when wrongs are committed is not "peace" either, but rather complacency and platitude.

"Peace" is not even absolute pacifism, which believes that violence is unjustifiable under any circumstances, even in self-defense. Absolute pacifism maintains that a person is not even to defend himself or herself when attacked. A nation is not to go to war against another nation for any reason, not even for self-defense and freedom. The reasoning is that if people refuse to fight, war would cease to exist. So pacifists are asked to refuse to obey orders for war, refuse to cooperate with war intentions, and to practice nonviolent resistance.

Relative pacifism does accept the concept of *just* war. Many argue that war is just when it is declared for a cause, by a legitimate authority, as a last resort, and with a true sense of proportionality and a good probability of success. These criteria clearly underscore the idea that people should not ever initiate war, and if they are driven to a justifiable defensive war, they do it not by choice, but as a sad necessity. Even still, not wanting war does not necessarily lead to lasting peace.

Peace has to be more than an ideal or some timeless absolute. It has to be a reality that is lived here and now. What "ought to be" has to be aligned with what "is." High ideals can become the excuse to dissociate ourselves from the situation of the present moment. Peace is not just an ideal. It is a plausible, living reality.

No one wants to live in fear, yet we do. Sooner or later, fear begets violence, not peace. Martin Luther King, Jr., summarized peace in this way: "Through

Peace is a way of life, a journey toward truth and integrity.

violence you murder the hater, but you do not murder the hate." Forced peace is not peace at all.

If true peace is none of these things, what does it look like?

Peace is a tangible presence of truthfulness and authenticity. When presence replaces absence and the positive replaces the negative, new dynamic insights for establishing peaceful conditions in and around us emerge. Peace is a way of life, a choice, an activity, and a journey toward truth and integrity.

A general rule in psychology tells us that what we focus our mind upon tends to become our experience. Peace is no exception to this. Therefore, we are going to notice a big difference when we focus on the spiritual energies of harmony, love, and peace. Somehow a more balanced cooperation is created between heat and cold, sound and silence, heaven and earth, enmity and friendliness, and hostility and good will. The result is a sure emergence of an atmosphere of peace.

So let us ban from our minds the destructive patterns of disturbance, disease, bitterness, hatred, and limitations, and replace them with positive patterns of harmony, compassion, truth, creativity, and growth. Here are some examples of what we can include and exclude in our daily patterns to achieve true peace.

Peace Practices

- Learn to listen, understand, and appreciate others. Avoid complaints and criticism.
- Help others become the best they can be by allowing them to make their own decisions. Avoid giving unnecessary "orders."
- Practice gentle and calm behavior. Avoid violent words, images, and behaviors.
- Cultivate silence, prayer, and meditation. Avoid noise and loud voices and sounds.
- Tap into the positive energies of courage, acceptance, and love. Put aside negative emotions like fear, jealousy, and hatred.
- Have reverence for life in all its forms. Avoid threats and intimidations, blind fanaticism, and exclusive "isms."
- Share with all the blessings you have received. Avoid giving grief or distress to others.
- Give value and validity to others' opinions, and

acknowledge and honor them. Stop being "right" in every discussion and situation.

- Focus on ideals of truth, balance, harmony, and beauty. Try to eliminate some of the pressure you put on those around you.

This list and other similar lists are good steps for being at peace with oneself and radiating peace. Since thinking determines action, it is imperative to replace negative ways of thinking with positive ones.

True peace, however, also involves reaching out to others and taking the necessary steps to help those in need of food, adequate housing, sufficient medical care, and appropriate education.

"Peacemaking isn't something we ought to do in our spare time; it's something we need to do all the time. Action to alleviate world hunger (including that down the block) is peacemaking," as theologian Robert McAfee Brown wrote. "Whatever enhances the well-being of the human family is peacemaking, the spreading of shalom."

No one has articulated this aspect of peace better than Pope John Paul II in his 1979 *Address to the General Assembly of the United Nations* and also in his *World Day of Peace Message* of 1982:

Unconditional and effective respect for each person's inalienable rights is the necessary condition in order that peace may reign in a society. Vis-à-vis these basic rights, all others are in a way derivatory and secondary. In a society in which these rights are not protected, the very idea of universality is dead as soon as a small group of individuals set up for their own exclusive advantage a principle of discrimination whereby the rights and even the lives of others are made dependent on the whim of the stronger.

Justice must be at the core of human rights and of peace. *Gaudium et Spes* of the Second Vatican Council states explicitly that peace "is rightly and appropriately called 'an enterprise of justice' (Isa 32:7). Peace results from that harmony built into human society by its Founder, and actualized by people who thirst after ever greater justice" (78).

Peace is a continuous process, for it is, in *Gaudium et Spes'* terms, "never attained once and for all, but must be built up ceaselessly" (78). This peace comes with continuously allowing God's grace to permeate our souls, with continuously striving for ever more harmony with others, with understanding, and good will. It comes with continuously trying to reach the contentment, order, and wholeness we really want, need, and long for. It has been said, and rightly so, that "Peace with God, peace with each other, and peace with ourselves come in the same package."

Peace also involves truth, creativity, and commitment. It is not the result of "pacifying" others by giving them drugs, keeping them illiterate and uniformed, unjustly invading their space and psyche, or keeping them in blind submission. Genuine peace seeks the truth wherever it is and awakens creativity. It finds inventive ways to cultivate activities that create structures for peace at all levels of our society.

Peace is not just for other peoples, other times, and other places. Peace is for here and now more than ever before. When physicist Robert Oppenheimer (1904–1967), the chairman of the Advisory Committee of the U.S. Atomic Energy Commission, was asked to appear before a Congressional Committee to answer whether or not there was any defense against the atomic bomb, he replied: "Certainly." "And that is?" someone asked. The audience held its breath until the eminent scientist replied softly, "Peace."

There is no alternative to peace. Peace begins with you and me, right here, right now. It leads us to "the way, and the truth, and the life" (Jn 14:6) that empowers us by granting us new hearts and the higher consciousnesses that war and violence achieve nothing. In peace's light, we realize that all of us are brothers and sisters on one earth and in one universe. Above all, we realize that we are soldiers in the same army—the army of the Prince of Peace.

For Your Reflection & Response

1. Do thoughts of anger, bitterness, resentment, or revenge from your past dictate your behavior? In what ways does this affect your daily living? Is there someone in your life you cannot forgive? Do you feel open to the idea of letting go of past hurts to be at peace with yourself and others? How might you begin this process?

2. Are you truthful in your words and actions when you deal with others? Have you ever damaged the reputation of someone through gossip or lies? What have you done to remedy this? How do you characterize your relationships with others, especially the members of your

family, friends, and coworkers? Do you show them respect and love? Do they reciprocate respect and love to you?

3. Socrates said, "I am not an Athenian, nor a Greek, but a citizen of the world." How, in your opinion, can a person be a "patriotic citizen" of a particular country and at the same time a "citizen of the world"? Can you be both at the same time, or would you feel forced to choose one over the other? Why does this matter? How might it affect peace in our world?

4. Although war has occasionally provided liberation, order, and justice, do such merits, in your opinion, justify war? Can you think of other ways to achieve the same results without the horrors of war? Abraham Lincoln said, "I destroy my enemies when I make them my friends." Is this a practical way to deal with our international enemies? Why or why not? On a personal level, what practical steps can you take to create bonds of friendship between you and your "enemies"? Have you tried any of these steps? How can you begin today?

5. If you were an adviser to the president, would you advise him to sign more peace and develop-

ment treaties with other countries? Or to withdraw from such treaties, arguing that the best defense should be based on nuclear deterrence? Would you advocate "security" through possessing more weapons or fewer weapons? What strategy for lasting peace would you recommend?

AFFIRMATION

Repeat this several times a day.

My consciousness of peace
supports me in being
in harmony with everyone
in my life.

Prayer

Dear God,

Reveal yourself to me, O God, as you really are—the God of love and peace. Grant me to be at peace with myself, with others, and with you.

Remind me that the things that provoke animosity with others are petty and trivial, and that I should treat them as such.

Set my heart and mind on your words so that I can be a dependable instrument for your message to others—the message of love and peace.

Dear God, I do not know what I shall become; but this I know: I want to be a person of peace. Since you have told us repeatedly not to be afraid (Mt 14:27, 17:7, 28:19), I will cast out all fear, for you are with me. I will not be afraid of peace.

Grant me the gifts of prudence, wisdom, understanding, and true friendship, so that I can journey along with others on the road of justice, freedom, respect, and love—the road that leads to lasting peace.

Grant me true and lasting peace, your peace, which is the bond of all genuine relationships. Amen.

CHAPTER THREE

Prophetic Peace

"Now may the Lord of peace himself give you peace at all times in all ways."

■ 2 THESSALONIANS 3:16

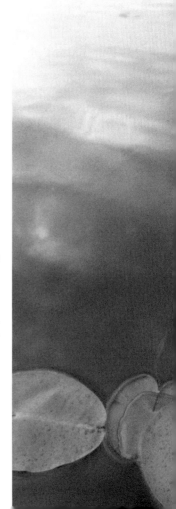

Violence does not just happen. It does not surface from nowhere. It does not come out of the blue. Violence takes place in the minds and hearts of human beings—which is where peace should take place as well.

The outside is always a reflection of the inside. Inner peace has great impact upon outer peace. Peace on the earth embodies the peace that is in the heaven of our minds, hearts, and souls.

43

Inner Peace

Inner peace is the result of the unity of the whole person—soul, mind, heart, and body—unity encompassing ideas, feelings, intuitions, convictions, and all that makes a person, a person. This unity goes as far as reaching the deeper areas of the soul that define our very relationship with God, which is guided by the divine lights of truth. In this very core of our being, God becomes the common ground of all beings and the source of unity for the whole person. Although the unity that produces inner peace is an end in itself, it is also a means to draw others to it. When achieved, treaties or political arrangements become superfluous.

No genuine peace can endure when it is the fruit of fear or when imposed by force. This is why Dietrich Von Hildebrand (1889–1977)—philosopher, spiritual writer, and anti-Nazi crusader—can write insightfully:

This inward peace, then, is infinitely more important even than all outward concord; however, it is not separable from the latter, but engenders it of necessity. If inward peace reigns in a man's soul—as it does in the saints'—it removes from any struggle he may have to wage the venoms of asperity and irritation, of harshness and malicious enmity. With him, the struggle for the kingdom of God becomes visibly and tangibly a struggle of peace against peacelessness.

When we reach such a deep level of inner peace, conflicts resolve themselves. Indeed, a deeper understanding of ourselves impels us to have a better understanding of our opponents. Perhaps their motivations are the same as ours after all. They may feel as right and righteous, courageous and patriotic, and well-intentioned and eager for peace as we feel. And if their motivations are simply based on evil, what evidence do we have to prove it? The bottom line is this: we may be creating and continuing to create the conflict without knowing that we are doing it.

At a deeper level, we mirror the "enemy" and the "enemy" mirrors us. We project whatever we dislike in ourselves onto others, and they do exactly the same to us. Unconsciously, what motivates our opponents is in us and runs, to a certain extent, our behavior. When we reach this level of understanding, there is a good chance that conflicts will dissolve. A trans-

> Very often we create conflict without even knowing we are doing it.

formation will take place on both sides, or, without a doubt, at least on one side.

In order to reach such an optimistic result, two conditions are necessary. The first one is that no matter what the conflict, we should abide in a state of inner peace—whole and with an eye totally focused on the source of all unity. The second condition is that we should always have in mind that our fight is against evil, not evildoers. Let us not forget that saints were sinners, too. St. Paul became the champion of faith *after* he was the champion of persecution.

Violence within us is the source of violence outside us.

In other words, when we are well-balanced inside, we should be able to identify the real enemy. If we lose our objective, or if we lose our inner balance, our peacemaking efforts will suffer greatly and will most likely fail.

Those who have worked with their inner lives are amazed to learn what impact resentment, anger, and bitterness have had within them, as well as in their relationships with others. Violence within us is the source of violence outside of us, and this can reach, if we are in positions of responsibility, the national and the international levels. We spend much time trying to shift attention to where the problem is not, because we are afraid of our own reality and we do not want to admit it. Deep down, we are afraid of the hidden reality—our own demons—and do anything that prevents us from facing them. But, we cannot hide who we really are for very long.

The well-being of the planet and all that lives on it depends on the very way we handle our feelings, perceptions, and consciousness.

There is another component to inner peace, which is to set our priorities right and take a hard look at what in us keeps the kingdom of God from coming, even though we pray everyday, "Your kingdom come" (Mt 6:10).

Are we really committed to work first for the values of the kingdom of God or, instead, do we allow our lives to reflect a primary commitment to the kingdom of money, power, prestige, pleasure, ideology, or any other substitute for God? What are the deep desires of our heart? Jesus warned us: "Where your treasure is, there your heart will be also" (Mt 6:21). Therefore "store up for yourselves treasures in heaven" (Mt 6:20). Sometimes, we forget that God is not only infinite power, but also infinite love; and that love is the greatest power of all. Love is the "constitution" by which the kingdom of God is ruled. The power of love can dissolve the power of war. The power of love is by far stronger than the love of power. As no darkness can resist a sparkle of light, so it is with war and love; no war can resist the power of love.

> Our own personal lives should be part of the peace-making pattern.

With love, we can overcome the most dangerous enemy, which dwells in ourselves. No, the "evil empire" may not always be out there in someone else; it can also be much closer to home—in our own hearts. We cannot live in peace if we are subject to our instincts, lusts, jealousies, hatreds, and ambitions. These have the power to generate weapons of mass destruction. We may be our worst enemy and we do not know it. The roots of enmity are not found in blood test results or DNA readings, but in hearts and minds.

Therefore, let us not be surprised by the violence emerging from peoples who are oppressed, hungry, homeless, lonely, uneducated, and have nothing to lose. Let us look honestly at the root causes of their problems and work on solving them.

Richard Rohr, commenting on war, wrote:

[People] love war so much that they are willing to believe lies, and even blatant lies to justify their need to export evil elsewhere, instead of dealing with it here….*We always avoid the inner conflict of good and evil, and externalize and dramatize it out there* (Rohr's emphasis). That is exactly the lie of redemptive violence that Jesus came to free us from.

When we free ourselves from our inner lies and readjust our priorities, we will begin to heal and heal the world with us. Peace, then, will emerge as a natural consequence.

There is no way to achieve world peace unless there is peace in peoples' hearts. This is why a comprehensive study in philosophy, religion, psychology, and other human sciences and development should be part of our education curricula. As always, inward journeys shape outward journeys.

History books usually report the beginning and end dates of a war. But these dates are not necessarily accurate because the war had already started in someone's mind long before the given date. Thich Nhat Hanh—world-renowned writer, poet, scholar, and Zen Buddhist monk—wrote: "Stopping the war in our minds and in our hearts, we will surely know how to stop the war outside." He also wrote these piercing lines:

> Violence is never far. It is possible to identify the seeds of violence in our everyday thoughts, speech, and actions. We can find these seeds in our own minds, in our attitudes, and in our fears and anxieties about ourselves and others. Thinking itself can be violent, and violent thoughts can lead us to speak and act violently. In this way, the violence in our minds manifests itself in the world.

This means that our own personal lives should be part of the peacemaking pattern. When we are a radiating center of peace, everything around us is influenced by our calm, collected, and poised attitude, even if we are not aware of it. Genuine peace moves us all along the road of transformation.

The heart of peace is the peace of the heart because, as author John Dear, S.J., put it,

> Nonviolence is the Spirit of God that disarms our hearts so that we can become God's instruments for the disarmament of the world. This nonviolent Spirit of God transforms us so as to transform the world.

Tips for Peacemaking

When we realize that genuine peace is of critical importance for our personal well-being and development, as well as for the well-being and development of the entire world, and that the latter is the natural result of the former, we find ourselves walking the road of a more peaceful life. Here are twenty action tips that will help achieve such a noble goal:

1. Set aside time daily to recall your blessings. Prayerfully reflect on all the good things God has given you.

2. See the other person's better nature and focus on the positive. Angry and brutal people also have qualities that can touch hearts. Draw their attention to the fact that their hostility is inconsistent with the kind of person they wish to be.

3. Let go of negative emotions. Let go of your hurts. Forgive and go on with your life. Ask those you have hurt to forgive you, too. Drop completely from your vocabulary labels such as stupid, dummy, and idiot. Use and encourage others to use positive and uplifting words.

4. Do not let fear be used against you and do not use it against anyone else. Do not behave like a victim and do not victimize anyone else.

5. Express often your love for the members of your family and your friends.

6. Purify your motives and set a goal/mission for your life. Encourage others to do the same.

7. Associate yourself with friends who have positive attitudes. They will provide you with support and encouragement.

8. Make time for regular exercise. Never miss it. Eat the right foods without compromise. Get enough sleep. Stay physically fit. Taking care of yourself physically works positively in favor of your mental health, which is a good way to deal with problems such as stress and depression, which are a fertile soil for violence.

9. Develop an "emergency" response to help you deal with the anger of others. Take a deep breath before reacting, or count to ten, or drink a glass of water, or go for a walk before responding. Convince yourself that the reason you were attacked was not necessarily personal. Sometimes, the attacker is just insecure or weak, or you just happen to be in the wrong place at the wrong time. Do not always take it seriously or personally.

10. Avoid judging. Never appear arrogant. Respect others and display equality with them. Let go of the need to be right; it is irrelevant to God's love and kingdom.

11. Do not underestimate the use of humor. Laughter releases embarrassment, reduces tension, allows a problem to be seen in a different perspective, and helps create a mood in which hopefulness and zest for life can emerge. Laughter helps much in the healing process.

12. When you are wrong, do not hesitate to apologize. The "I'm sorry" phrase should not hurt your pride. Rather, it helps wipe away the pain of the hurt you have caused. The world would be a more peaceful place if people admitted the wrongs they do, apologized for them, and corrected their behaviors.

13. Never say things about others that you will not be able to say directly to their faces. Never listen to gossip, and if you somehow feel obligated to listen, never repeat it.

14. Beware of prejudices. We may not like to admit it, but we are not completely free of them. They usually are based on race, gender, age, socioeco-

nomic status, religious affiliation, political preference, or national origin. Prejudices cause anger, frustration, and despair. Always separate the person from a problem or issue. Respect the right to be different and beware of labeling anyone.

15. Listen, listen, and listen. Deep listening allows others to speak out, even if what they say contains errors, wrong perceptions, blame, or resentment. By listening with compassion, you may lose an enemy, win a friend, and go one step forward on the road to a more peaceful life.

16. In your discussions with others, reveal your underlying values, assumptions, experiences, doubts, fears, and personal commitments. These may add more authenticity and truth to a relationship.

17. Express your conviction about peace verbally or in writing. You can also express peace with other tools such as music, drama, visual arts/crafts. Say it, sing it, play it, paint it, shape it.

18. Talking about peace is good, but it is not enough. You have to commit to, work for, and promote what you stand for. If a culture of peace is what we want, everyone—you and I before anyone

else—should work untiringly to achieve it. Keep in mind what political philosopher Edmund Burke (1729–1797) said: "All that is necessary for the triumph of evil is that good men do nothing." Also, Martin Luther King, Jr. said: "Men for years now have been talking about war and peace. But, now, no longer can they just talk about it. It is no longer a choice between violence and nonviolence in this world, it's nonviolence or non-existence."

Pray, meditate, and ask for the gift of peace.

19. Join an active local or national organization that works on peace issues. Write letters to officials in government, to editors of newspapers and magazines, and convince them to endorse peace policies. Sow and water the seeds of understanding, compassion, and nonviolence. If you transform your consciousness, and I transform mine, we will make a significant contribution toward the change of the collective consciousness. A nation will change when you and I change. The world will change when our nation and other nations change.

20. All this cannot be done properly without divine help. So let God be involved in your life. Pray, meditate, and ask for the gift of peace. You only know that you have this gift when you share it. Peace is by its very nature a shared experience.

Urgency for a Culture of Peace

Albert Einstein once said:

> The release of atomic energy has created a new world in which old ways of thinking, that include old diplomatic conventions and balance-of-power politics, have become utterly meaningless. Mankind must give up war in the atomic era. What is at stake is the life or death of humanity.

We can no longer afford to make mistakes when it comes to the issues of war and peace, especially in an era of weapons of mass destruction. Your destiny, my destiny, and the destiny of the entire planet is at stake, and it would be foolish to just surrender to those who cannot dissociate themselves from old ways of thinking. Though they may be well-intentioned, sincere, courageous, and dedicated to their duties, their dependency on weapons as a threat is unacceptable today. The Second Vatican Council underscored the revolutionary character of the modern world in these terms:

> The living conditions of modern people have been so profoundly changed in their social and cultural dimensions, that we can speak of a new age in human history. Fresh avenues are open, therefore, for the refinement and the wider diffusion of culture. These avenues have been paved by the enormous growth of natural, human, and social sciences, by progress in technology, and by advances in the development and organization of the means by which people communicate with one another (*Gaudium et Spes*, 54).

The virus of terrorism has already spread worldwide while we are wasting time with short-sighted, self-interested policies. We may win, and we will certainly win this battle or that battle, using our most sophisticated weapons. But how will we eradicate evil? A new way of thinking is the only hope for winning the final battle.

A culture of peace in which everyone wins is needed. A higher consciousness that declares the needlessness of all wars should awaken every person to contribute to this cause. A collective spiritual consciousness is on the rise, and that's good news.

Today we know as never before that we are all in the same boat and we have to survive the same storms. We are all brothers and sisters, responsible for each other, as *Gaudium et Spes* says,

> Thus we are witnesses of the birth of a new humanism, one in which we are defined first of all by our responsibility toward our brothers and sisters and toward history (55).

Pacifist A. J. Muste (1885–1967) says: "War is not an accident. It is the logical outcome of a certain way of life. If we want to attack war, we have to attack that way of life." We have to work on the root causes of violence, rather than its symptoms.

This means that we should work on revising our educational curricula to include values and behaviors that promote a culture of peace. We should work for justice and equality for all, by eradicating discrimination of any kind. We should foster economic and social development everywhere. We should underscore the respect for human rights everywhere and always, and promote understanding, tolerance, solidarity, and other human qualities. We should develop good communication through dialogue and respect between individuals and between nations, and settle conflicts through negotiations and good will that benefit all sides. And in time of conflict, we should use it constructively, by securing the right balance between independence and interdependence, in order to produce better alternatives than either conflicting party could have produced alone.

A culture of peace is a dynamic, active, and continuous process. It calls for constant, intentional, and organic change, day by day, habit by habit, attitude by attitude, individual by individual, group by group, and nation by nation.

A culture of peace is not a simple thing. It is complex, and sometimes very complex because we ourselves are very complex and diverse. Peace is part of a comprehensive process that involves becoming fully human as individuals and as a community. This is a massive undertaking. It is sad that our educational system ignores this process. It is concerned more with producing skilled graduates than with producing fully human persons. It does not pay enough attention to health, wholeness, and integrity, which are essential for the development of the whole person. In our present system, one may reach a high level of skills for a

> A culture of peace is a dynamic, active, and continuous process.

particular job, but is not well-educated because he or she does is not focused on the fullness of life.

"Love one another" (Jn 15:12) and "Your kingdom come" (Mt 6:10) mean (besides almsgiving, which is good but not enough) paying closer attention to all the needs of the whole person, physically, mentally, and spiritually. Peace is not an abstract concept or agreement about how things are supposed to be. It is a daily living reality. It is dynamic and focused. It affects every aspect of human life. It is a prescription for well-being. Peace is the way to the fullness of life.

Jesus brought to the world the reality of unconditional love—God's unconditional love for us and ours for God and for one another. Unconditional love does not say: "I love you, if you do this or that." It says: "I love you no matter what because you are the child and image of God and because we are one in God."

Because such love is possible, we dare to hope for true peace within us and in the entire world; a peace that allows us to become fully human, the way God intends us to be. Does this sound idealistic or even impossible? Perhaps, but Jesus, who promised to be with us "always, until the end of the world" (Mt 28:20), also said, "What is impossible for mortals is possible for God" (Lk 18:29).

For Your Reflection & Response

1. Are you involved in building a healthy spirituality for yourself and the people around you? If not, would you be willing to pursue a degree, or do research, or just help in critical areas of self-development and the development of your surroundings? In your opinion, how important is an attitude of nonviolence in contributing to your own healing and the healing of the world? What practical steps can you take to reach this goal? Are you at peace with every member of your own family and with every other person with whom you are in contact? If not, why not? Do you make every effort to restore peace when conflict arises? Does this effort contribute in healing you and the other person?

2. Victor Hugo (1802–1885) said: "Civil war? What does that mean? Is there any foreign war? Isn't every war fought between men, between brothers?" Isn't every war caused by what people carry inside themselves: fanaticism, revenge, anger, injustice, humiliation, or greed? What would be, in your opinion, the reason for violence if we are at peace within ourselves?

3. Why do people seem attracted to violence more than to peace? Why do we love violence on TV and in movies? Why do we need enemies? Do enemies teach us something? Do you think wars are inevitable? Do you think poverty, injustice, humiliation, lack of understanding, ignorance, greed, emotional unbalance, and stupidity can also be reasons for war? Is reason alone sufficient for the resolution of conflicts? Do you think a nonviolent world is possible? Why, or why not?

4. What is your reaction to George Bernard Shaw's assertion that "Patriotism is your conviction that this country is superior to all others because you were born in it"? What is your own definition of patriotism? Is patriotism an asset or an obstacle to peace in the world? Name both the strengths and weaknesses of a nationalistic approach to war and peace.

5. What role does the arms industry, the entertainment industry, and the media play in promoting the culture of violence? Why do peace movements often arouse suspicions among both the well-to-do and working classes? Is peace always perceived as a radical alternative?

How do you see it? After reading this book, what practical things can you do to add another stone to the edifice of peace?

AFFIRMATION

Repeat this several times a day.

I am radiating God's peace in the world.

PRAYER

Dear God,

Deep, at the very center of my being where you dwell, let me find peace.

In the integration of my soul, mind, heart, and body, let me be at peace.

Gently, in the intimate circle of my family and friends, and any person I meet today, let me share peace.

Lovingly, in the larger circle of humankind that includes all those who wish me ill, let me radiate peace.

Be the solution of my inner "civil wars" and contradictions, and don't allow me to choose the path of suspicion, hatred, and confusion, for you are "a God not of disorder but of peace" (1 Cor 14:33).

Let us human beings use our science and every knowledge we have for creativity and peace and not for destruction.

Help us love one another, never deceive one another, despise one another, or use one another.

Let every one of us bloom in peace.

Let every one of us be a healing peace for others.

"Let there be peace on earth, and let it begin with me." Amen.

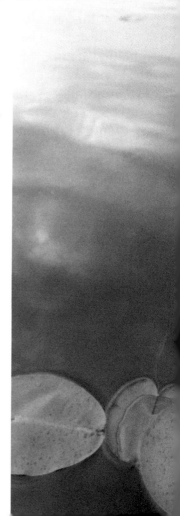

One person at a time—starting with oneself—can bring more security, safety, and sanity to the world.

Some people commit acts of violence in the name of God, or for a cause such as self-cultural protection, honor, or spiritual values. When they die for this or that cause, they are declared martyrs.

No one doubts that people who are attacked have the right to defend themselves. They certainly should. But how? If they choose to attack the attackers with a more devastating force, thinking that by eliminating these evildoers, they eliminate evil, they will be disappointed, as history has shown.

65

All the wars of human history have not removed a single molecule of hatred from the human heart.

Such a strategy may bring remedy to the symptoms, but not to the illness itself. Evil has been here since Adam and Eve, Cain and Abel, Ishmael and Isaac, East/West and North/South confrontations, and every other conflict imaginable. The devastating events of September 11, 2001, and all that followed have proved in the most spectacular way that no military strength, economic power, or advanced technology is able to guarantee security or transform hearts.

All the wars of human history have not removed a single molecule of hatred from the human heart.

There must be a way to kill the virus of violence without killing the violent. Wasn't St. Paul "the persecutor" par excellence? He became the champion, propagator, and martyr for the very cause he was fighting, and the very people he was persecuting.

The mystery of life cannot be understood outside our relationship with God—the source of life. Only this determines the set of values we should live by, war and peace included.

A new consciousness—a transformation in Christ—involves harmony, a concord of hearts, rejection of all forms of violence, and a hope for real peace as described by the prophet: "The wolf shall live with the lamb, the leopard shall lie down with the kid, the calf and the lion and the fatling together, and a little child shall lead them" (Isa 11:6).

This vision is possible only when we place our trust in God and ask that God's promise will be fulfilled:

> A new heart I will give you and a new spirit I will put within you; and I will remove from your body the heart of stone and give you a heart of flesh. I will put my spirit within you, and make you follow my statutes and be careful to observe my ordinances (Ezek 36:26–27).

In human terms, peace is practically impossible. Not so in divine terms. "What is impossible for mortals is possible for God" (Lk 18:27).

When we receive the peace of Christ and cry out with St. Paul, "It is no longer I who live, but it is Christ who lives in me" (Gal 2:20), our outlook on life will be radically different and it will affect the decisions we make. We want to hate sin not the sinners, eradicate it in us first, and bring all others along with us to a closer relationship with God—the source of true and lasting peace.

The new outlook will also affect the way we live in the world. We will be sensitive to the needs of others more than to our own needs. We want them to see in us the Christ they don't see. Kindness, forgiveness, compassion, and understanding will show them the Christ who is alive and who is the secret of our peace.

A new era of human civilization should be the common goal to which each one of us has the duty to contribute. We are talking about a true new world order here, a "New humanity" (Eph 2:15), a "New creation" (Gal 6:15), and the "Kingdom of God" (Mt 6:33; Mk 1:15).

Christ consciousness brings about the kingdom of God and the peace on earth, so longed for by every heart.